TABLE OF CONTENTS

Legal Disclaimer — 3

About this Planner — 4

Budget Spreadsheet & Video Tutorial — 5

Glossary of Financial Terms — 6

Section I
Let's Get Organized (Expenses, Debt, & Income) — 8

Section II
Debt Management (Creating a Debt Management Plan) — 14

Section III
The Budget (Making Your Money Work For You) — 21

Section IV
Goal Setting — 30

LEGAL DISCLAIMER

The Melanin Project, LLC and its coaches are financial and budget consultants. They are not investment advisors or tax advisors. The information and material contained within this planner is for informational purposes. The Melanin Project, LLC and its coaches make no representations or warrantees the effectiveness of their recommendations. The reader is solely responsible for the reader's outcome. Financial and budget planning advice is given by The Melanin Project, LLC without any guarantee of particular results or its effectiveness with the readers individual situation.

All rights reserved. No parts of this publication may be reproduced, stored in a retrieval system or transmitted in any form by any means (including electronic, mechanical, photocopying, recording, or otherwise) without prior written permission from The Melanin Project, LLC.

ABOUT THIS PLANNER

Welcome to our Budget Planner, your essential tool for financial empowerment and control. Managing your finances is a crucial aspect of achieving your financial goals and securing a stable future. This user-friendly budget planner is designed to simplify the often daunting task of budgeting, providing you with a strategic and practical approach to taking charge of your money.

At its core, budgeting is about understanding your income, expenses, and spending patterns. Our Budget Planner is here to guide you through this process, helping you create a realistic and achievable financial plan. Whether you're aiming to save for a big purchase, pay off debt, or simply gain a better understanding of your financial landscape, this tool is your ally in the journey towards financial success.

The Budget Planner offers a comprehensive yet straightforward interface, allowing you to input your income, categorize your expenses, and set realistic spending limits. Visualizing your financial situation is a powerful step towards making informed decisions and taking control of your money. This tool empowers you to identify areas where you can save, plan for future expenses, and allocate resources wisely.

Your financial journey is unique, and our Budget Planner recognizes that. It's customizable to fit your specific needs and goals. Whether you're a seasoned budgeter or just starting on this financial adventure, our Budget Planner is designed to accommodate users of all levels of expertise.

Get ready to embark on a journey of financial clarity and control. Use our Budget Planner to pave the way for a more secure and prosperous financial future. Your financial goals are within reach, and this planner is your trusted companion on the path to achieving them.

BUDGET SPREADSHEEET & VIDEO TUTORIALS

Streamline Your Finances with a Budget Tool

- We are delighted to present our exclusive budget spreadsheet, available in both Google Sheets and Excel formats!

- To create and manage your budget effectively, we recommend using a computer-based budget spreadsheet. Unlike traditional paper, a budget spreadsheet allows you to make changes more efficiently. However, we understand that not everyone prefers spreadsheets, but you can still complete your budget without one.

- Download your free premium budget tool at:
  themelaninproject.gumroad.com/l/byligu/budget100

Video Tutorials

- Unlock additional knowledge with our accompanying video tutorials, enriching your experience with this planner! Dive deeper into key topics, ensuring you master every aspect of budgeting and financial planning. These tutorials serve as invaluable supplements, offering step-by-step guidance.

- As a bonus, we've included extra content to further elevate your financial journey. From insider tips to advanced strategies, consider this our gift to you. Embrace a holistic approach to financial empowerment — explore, learn, and conquer your financial goals with confidence.

- If you see the image above this indicates that a video is available for more detailed instruction. Watch the video tutorials at:
  themelaninproject.gumroad.com/l/tprus/personalfinance200

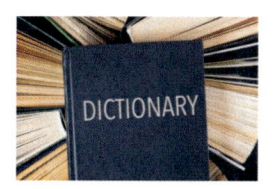

SECTION V
GLOSSARY OF TERMS

This collection of terms is a handy resource that will aide you in understanding some of the financial concepts listed within this budget planner. Provided terms are not an all inclusive list of financial terms as this list focuses specifically on the budgeting process discussed within.

Term	Explanation
Budget	A plan that outlines what money you expect to earn or receive (your income) and how you will save it or spend it (your expenses) for a given period of time; also called a spending plan.
Debt	Money you owe another person or a business.
Debt Snowball	The debt snowball method is a debt-reduction strategy where you pay off debt in order of smallest to largest, gaining momentum as you knock out each remaining balance. When the smallest debt is paid in full, you roll the minimum payment you were making on that debt into the next-smallest debt payment.
Emergency Fund	A cash reserve that's specifically set aside for unplanned expenses or financial emergencies. Some common examples include car repairs, home repairs, medical bills, or a loss of income.
Expenses	The cost required for something; the money spent on something.

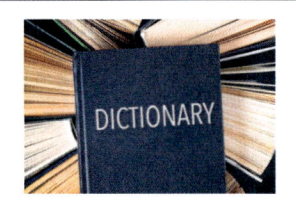

SECTION V
GLOSSARY OF TERMS

Term	Explanation
Generational Wealth	Wealth that is transferred from parents or relatives to children or other members of their family. This may take the form of cash, property, or anything else that has financial value, as well as investments in children's education, like paying for college or vocational training. Also referred to as intergenerational wealth.
Financial Literacy & Wealth Literacy	Financial literacy is what you need to know to be more financially successful than you otherwise could have been. Wealth literacy is the how you can put your knowledge to use to increased your net worth. Source: www.themedium.com
Income	Money earned or received such as wages or salaries, tips, commissions, contracted pay, government transfer payments, dividends on investments, tax refunds, gifts, and inheritances. Net income is the amount of money you receive in your paycheck after taxes and other deductions are taken out; also called take home pay.

Glossary of terms sourced from consumerfinance.gov unless source is specified under a specific term

SECTION I
LET'S GET ORGANIZED

Expenses, Debt Owed & Income

It's time to get organized. Before you get started with this section we would like to emphasize the importance of grasping where your money is going each month. As the slogan goes "if you don't know where your money is going it will leave you." Lets acknowledge that many people will avoid taking this very first step. However, this step is critical in getting you where you need to be. Not having a plan for your money can lead to devastating consequences. Learning to organize your financial house can help you learn to make your money work for you instead of you working for it. Section I provides several worksheets. These worksheets serve as prompters to ensure that you gather all necessary details to finalize your financial plan. Lets review the things you will need to gather:

- **Expenses:** How much do you pay per month? Use worksheet A to make note of this information. Monthly expenses includes things like utilities, rent, mortgage, car note, car expenses, child care, food, toiletries, phone, etc.

- **Debt Owed:** How much debt is owed? Use worksheet B to make note of total balance due, interest rate, minimum payment required for your debts. Debt includes things like balance owed for your mortgage, loans, credit card balances, health bills, etc.

- **Net Income:** Make note of all sources of income. How often do you get paid, and how much do you make after taxes and deductions are taken out. Use worksheet C to make note of your income.

WORKSHEET A
LIST MONTHLY EXPENSES HERE

Trim non-essential expenses. It's time to embrace new habits!

Due Date	Name of Bill	Monthly Payment	Late ??

WORKSHEET B
LIST MONTHLY DEBTS HERE

Ever thought about cutting back on TV and movie subscriptions? Shifting those funds to pay off debts can boost your financial journey!

Name of Creditor   Minimum Pymt   Amount Owed   Interest Rate

DID YOU MISS ANYTHING?

Below are some additional expense considerations you should keep in mind while constructing your financial plan.

EXPENSES ITEM	BUDGET	NOTES
MORTGAGE/RENT		
HOUSEHOLD MAINTENANCE		
TAXES		
INSURANCE		
ELECTRICITY		
WATER		
SEWAGE		
GAS		
PHONE		
TRASH		
CABLE		
CELL PHONE		
GROCERIES		
ENTERTAINMENT		
CHARITY/DONATIONS		
FUEL		
AUTO INSURANCE		
CAR PAYMENT		
CHILD CARE		
CREDIT CARDS/DEBT		
LOANS		
DINING OUT		
SPORTING EVENTS		
LIVE THEATER		
CONCERTS		
MOVIES		
GYM MEMBMBERSHIP		

WORKSHEET C

LIST YOUR SOURCES OF INCOME

Income Stream 1_____

Income Stream 2_____

Income Stream 3_____

Income Stream 4_____

Total Income_____

MAKE NOTE OF YOUR NEXT SIX PAY DATES

Pay date_____

Pay date_____

Pay date_____

Pay date_____

Pay date_____

Pay date_____

☑ CONGRATULATIONS ON GATHERING THE NEEDED DATA

Now Lets Get Ready To

- Declutter your life
- Pay off any bad debts
- Build an emergency fund and savings
- Improve your credit score
- Set some larger financial goals

SECTION II
MANAGING DEBT

Creating Your Debt Management Plan

After a full assessment of your financial state, including how much debt you owe and to whom. In Section II, we can now begin the process of creating a debt management plan. Organizing and managing debt can be a daunting task for anyone. With the increasing cost of living, credit card debt, student loan debt, and other debt mounting, it's important to have a plan in place to help you keep track of your finances and work towards paying down your debt. Organizing and managing debt can be overwhelming, but fortunately there are plenty of tools, resources, and support available to help.

Finally, it's important to remember:

- You don't have to go through this process alone.
- The road to financial freedom can be difficult, but it doesn't have to be overwhelming. There are a variety of resources available to help, such as personal finance blogs, books, podcasts, or you might consider hiring a financial professional.
- Additionally, you can also seek out support from friends and family.

Don't rob yourself of your future by buying things to impress other people as this will make you poor. Use debt to buy assets and not toys and liabilities. Learn to live within your means.

14

SECTION II
MANAGING DEBT

Creating Your Debt Management Plan using FAST

Lets take a closer look at the FAST approach for debt management planning. To create an effective debt management plan, we employ a comprehensive method called FAST. This approach helps you organize your debts to pay them off as fast as possible, leaving more funds in your monthly budget for other expenses. To make the most of this plan, it's essential to stick to it. Let's break down what FAST stands for:

F — Focus on high priority debts first

A — Assess and allocate your monthly budget towards debt payments

S — Settle your debts methodically

T — Track your progress and adjust the plan if needed

FAST METHOD

Debt Management Plan
FAST #

We will use the FAST method and worksheet B to sequence the payoff for every debt you listed. If you'd prefer, you can also do this digitally using Excel or Google Sheets. Otherwise, we provided a blank template on page 18 of this planner for you to finalize your FAST sequence. Next we will identify your FAST #. Here is how to come up with the FAST #.

Example: Take ABC Store's balance and divide it by the minimum payment due each month. That number is the Fast # for that creditor. Lets break that down numerically: Take $2,294 divided by $25 = **91.76** This means that it will take approximately **92** payments to pay off ABC Store assuming you only paid the minimum payment due. Notice that we rounded the number up.

Take some time to practice and/or watch the video tutorial as needed to ensure you understand how FAST works. We have provided the answers to the rest of the sequence below.

Creditor	Balance	Minimum Payment	Interest Rate	Fast #	Fast Ranking
ABC Store Credit Card	$2,294	$25	2%	92	
Student Loan	$32,000	$200	3.5%	160	
Ralphs Credit Card	$5,536	$67	27%	83	
Car Loan	$13,286	$275	6%	48	
Ryan's Furniture Credit Card	$972.36	$80	15%	12	

FAST METHOD

Debt Management Plan
FAST Ranking

Now that the number of payments needed to pay off each debt is known, it's time to finalize the FAST ranking. Find the lowest FAST # on the chart and rank it as 1. The rest can then be ranked from lowest to highest based on the Fast #. This information will help when creating a budget to pay down debt more quickly. Note that the FAST method does not emphasize interest rate, but sometimes the sequence may change depending on agreements with creditors; for instance, you might choose to pay off 0% interest debt first.

Example: Find the lowest FAST # on the chart below. That number is identified as 12. Because this debt would take the least amount of payments to pay off we will rank that creditor as 1.

Note that the debt management plan is an essential part of completing your financial plan. Your debt management plan will aide you in capturing more dollars back into your monthly budget. Thus allowing you to work down your debt much faster.

We have provided the answers to the rest of the sequence below. Take sometime to practice and then finalized your personal debt management plan. Watch the video tutorial as needed.

Creditor	Balance	Minimum Payment	Interest Rate	Fast #	Fast Ranking
ABC Store Credit Card	$2,294	$25	2%	92	4
Student Loan	$32,000	$200	3.5%	160	5
Ralphs Credit Card	$5,536	$67	27%	83	3
Car Loan	$13,286	$275	6%	48	2
Ryan's Furniture Credit Card	$972.36	$80	15%	12	1

FAST METHOD

Blank Tool

Calculate your overall balances and monthly minimum payments.

Creditor	Balance	Minimum Payment	Actual Payment	Interest Rate	Fast #	Fast Ranking

FAST METHOD

Blank Tool

Creditor	Balance	Minimum Payment	Actual Payment	Interest Rate	Fast #	Fast Ranking

FAST METHOD

Blank Tool

Creditor	Balance	Minimum Payment	Actual Payment	Interest Rate	Fast #	Fast Ranking

SECTION III
THE BUDGET

Making Your Money Work For You

TUTORIAL AVAILABLE

In this section, you will begin the process of creating your personal budget. The budget gives you an overview of where your money is going and will help you identify areas where you can make cuts. It allows you to identify your income, expenses, and savings goals, and create a plan to reach them. When you budget, you are in control of your finances, instead of letting them control you. If you are spending more than you earn, look for ways to reduce spending or increase your income. Paying off debt should also be a priority, as it will help to improve your credit score. As we develop your personal budget, we will show you how to incorporate your debt management plan into the process. In order to budget for success remember that:

- Budgeting is the key to unlocking financial freedom. It is the foundation of a successful and secure financial future. By properly managing your budget, you will be able to make wise financial decisions and have the confidence to achieve your goals. Budgeting is an important financial tool that can help you make the most of your money.

- Once you have your budget in place, you can start to save for the future. Start small, and create an emergency savings fund. Make sure you are contributing to your retirement savings as well. If you need help setting up a retirement account, talk to a banker, financial planner, an accountant, or your employer.

SECTION III
THE BUDGET

Making Your Money Work For You

- Finally, it's important to review your budget regularly. Sit down and assess your spending and make changes where necessary. This will help ensure that you are staying on track and will help you reach your financial goals. Overall, budgeting is an essential tool for keeping your finances under control. It takes some discipline and effort, but it is worth it in the end. By taking the time to create and manage a budget, you will have the security and freedom to pursue your goals. Lets start by discussing your emergency/savings fund.

Note: Automate your bills and monthly income
Automating your bills and monthly income is a game-changer in the world of budgeting and wealth-building. By setting up automatic payments, you not only streamline your financial responsibilities but also eliminate the risk of missing due dates. This ensures that your hard-earned money is allocated efficiently, preventing unnecessary late fees and maintaining a healthy credit score. In essence, automating bills isn't just a convenience; it's a strategic move that supports your budgeting efforts and lays the groundwork for building sustainable wealth.

In addition, direct deposit is the unsung hero on the path to wealth building. By automating the inflow of your income directly into your account, you eliminate the temptation to splurge before saving. This financial efficiency not only streamlines your budgeting process but also ensures that a portion of your earnings is consistently earmarked for savings and/or investments.

SECTION III
THE BUDGET

First Priority: Emergency & Savings

Emergency Fund

Having an emergency fund and savings is an incredibly important part of financial planning. It is a form of insurance that can help protect you from the unexpected, so that when a financial emergency arises, you have a cushion to fall back on.

An emergency fund is typically a portion of your savings that is earmarked for unexpected or emergency expenses, such as an expensive medical bill, the loss of a job, or a major home repair. Having an emergency fund gives you peace of mind that, even if something unexpected were to happen, you wouldn't be completely financially devastated.

Savings

Savings, on the other hand, are used to help fund your future goals and dreams. This could include saving for retirement, a vacation, a new car, a wedding, or a down payment on a house. Savings are also important for providing financial security. They can help protect your financial future, and give you options in case of an emergency.

23

SECTION III
THE BUDGET

First Priority: Emergency & Savings

Creating and maintaining an emergency fund and savings can be challenging. It is important to make sure you are setting aside money each month so that you are consistently build your savings. It is also important to make sure that your emergency fund is easily accessible. However, your emergency fund and savings should be kept in a separate bank account from your day to day expenditures to avoid spending triggers.

Overall, having an emergency fund and savings is a critical part of financial planning. With a little planning and effort, you can be confident that you have a financial safety net if something were to happen.

Note: Your Emergency Fund
Your first goal is to fund your emergency fund as quickly as possible. We recommend that you set aside $1000 dollars for an emergency.

SECTION III
THE BUDGET

Lets Review The Budget

Next, we will help you finalize your budget. Enclosed below is a preview of a monthly budget based on the information compiled from all of the worksheets. This is known as a reconciliation preview which shows all monthly expenses and income. Here are the steps you will take to finalize your budget using the monthly budget planner located on page 27 or your downloaded spreadsheet. For an example of how your monthly budget planner should look when completed you can preview a paper version on the next page or view the budget video tutorial for the spreadsheet view.

Date	Deposit Type	Planned Amount
3/1/2023	Pay Check 1	3,000.00
3/15/2023	Pay Check 2	3,000.00
Total		6,000.00

Due Date	Bills	Mar-2023
3-Mar	Rent	$1,200.00
5-Mar	Electric	$75.00
7-Mar	ABC Credit Card	$25.00
15-Mar	Student Loan	$200.00
16-Mar	Phone	$88.00
18-Jan	Ralphs Credit Card	$67.00
23-Mar	Ryans Funiture	$80.00
27-Mar	Car Note	$275.00
28th	Life Insurance	$26.00
29-Mar	Car Insurance	$97.00
	Food	$250.00
	Gas	$80.00
	Entertainment	$100.00
	Toiletries	$25.00
	Total	$2,588.00

Income - Expenses = **$3412**
$1000 goes directly to emergency fund
$2412 goes to FAST payments

- Add your income sources to the monthly budget planner worksheet provided. Total monthly income is **$6000**

- Add your expenses to the monthly budget planner worksheet provided. This includes expenses that are not always fixed like food, gas, etc. Total monthly expenses are: **$2588**

- Add your savings amount to your monthly budget planner worksheet. We recommend while learning new habits and starting the process to pay down debt that you allot 5% of your after tax income for savings. For this budget each pay period needs to allot $150. Total savings per month is: **$300** This $300 would go towards funding the emergency fund. However, our first goal is to fund the emergency fund with $100 as quickly as possible, which we have illustrated on the next page.

MONTHLY BUDGET PLANNER

EXAMPLE

NAME: JANE

MONTH: MARCH

INCOME

INCOME SOURCES	AMOUNT
PAYCHECK 1	$3000
PAYCHECK 2	$3000
TOTAL	$6000

SAVING GOAL/EMERGENCY FUND

ITEM	AMOUNT
EMERGENCY FUND	$1000
TOTAL	$1000

EXPENSES

EXPENSES ITEM	AMOUNT	DUE DATE
RENT	$1200.00	3/3
ELECTRIC	$75.00	3/5
ABC CREDIT CARD	$25.00	3/7
STUDENT LOAN	$200.00	3/15
PHONE	$88.00	3/16
RALPHS CREDIT CARD	$67.00	3/18
RYANS FURNITURE	$80.00	3/23
CAR NOTE	$275.00	3/27
LIFE INSURANCE	$26.00	3/28
CAR INSURANCE	$97.00	3/29
FOOD	$250.00	
GAS	$80.00	
ENTERTAINMENT	$100.00	
TOILETRIES	$25.00	
TOTAL	$2588	

MONTHLY SUMMARY

TOTAL INCOME	TOTAL EXPENSES	DIFFERENCE
$6000	$2588	$3412

FAST PAYMENT *FAST*
$2412

Notes: Notice that we subtracted $1000 for the emergency fund

MONTHLY
BUDGET PLANNER

NAME:

MONTH:

INCOME

INCOME SOURCES	AMOUNT
TOTAL	

SAVING GOAL/EMERGENCY FUND

ITEM	AMOUNT
TOTAL	

EXPENSES

EXPENSES ITEM	AMOUNT	DUE DATE
	TOTAL	

MONTHLY SUMMARY

TOTAL INCOME	TOTAL EXPENSES	DIFFERENCE

FAST PAYMENT	NOTES

SECTION III
THE BUDGET

HABITS, MINDSET, & TRIGGERS

| HABITS | MINDSET | TRIGGERS |

Habits

Forming good financial habits is essential in order to be successful and secure in the long run. It is very important to have a positive attitude and mindset towards money, as well as an understanding of the basics of money management. Good financial habits can improve overall financial well-being and help to prevent financial difficulties in the future. These habits and mindset should be developed early on, and should be continually practiced in order to gain the most benefit.

MINDSET

The mindset associated with money is also very important. Having a positive attitude towards money and finances can make the difference between achieving success or being a failure. Having a mindset of abundance as opposed to scarcity is important. This involves believing that there is enough money to go around and that it can be used to create a better life.

EMBRACE ABUNDANCE

Actions speak louder than intentions. It's through consistent habits that we transform prayers and meditations into tangible results.

SECTION III
THE BUDGET

HABITS, MINDSET, & TRIGGERS

| HABITS | MINDSET | TRIGGERS |

It is also important to look at money as a tool, and not an end goal or something to be worshipped. Having a good financial mindset involves taking responsibility for money and making smart choices. Having a good financial mindset requires being disciplined and organized. Being financially empowered, understanding the basics of financial planning, setting realistic goals, and having a plan are all essential to having a good financial mindset.

Being aware of financial triggers is a big part of mindset, and habits. Trying to keep up with the lifestyles of friends, family, and spending money on things that are not aligned with the goals you have established can impact your ability to master your budget and build wealth. Sometimes triggers can be related to our past history of trauma. If you feel as though your trauma history is impacting your spending habits. We encourage you to connect with a licensed professional for support.

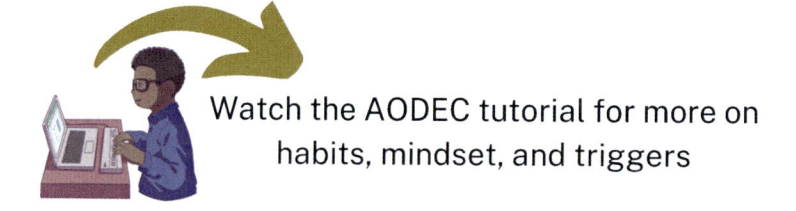

Watch the AODEC tutorial for more on habits, mindset, and triggers

SECTION III
THE BUDGET

TUTORIAL AVAILABLE

FAST

How to Apply Your Fast Payment

Lets talk about how to use your FAST payment. Now that all monthly expenses are organized and the emergency fund has been addressed. Left over funds should be utilized to pay off debts. Jane has **$2412** left over in her bank account and has enough funds to pay off her Ryan's Furniture credit card for $972.36 and $1439.64 would go towards her car loan. Notice that Jane has a $13,286 dollar car loan balance. Jan would continue to pay her monthly car loan payment as scheduled and the $1439.64 would go towards the remaining balance. This is one of the reasons why we call it the FAST method.

Within the first month, Jane was able to capture $80 back in her monthly budget, pay off $2412 worth of debt, pay off one creditor, and also funded her emergency fund.

Creditor	Balance	Minimum Payment	Interest Rate	Fast #	Fast Ranking
ABC Store Credit Card	$2,294	$25	2%	92	4
Student Loan	$32,000	$200	3.5%	160	5
Ralphs Credit Card	$5,536	$67	27%	83	3
Car Loan	$13,286	$275	6%	48	2
Ryan's Furniture Credit Card	$972.36	$80	15%	12	1

SECTION IV
SETTING FINANCIAL GOALS

Why Are Financial Goals Important?

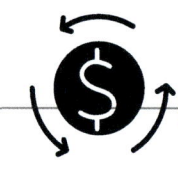

Direction

Financial goals provide direction and meaning. They make it easier for you to make sacrifices or stick to a budget because you know what outcome you're striving for. They help you keep focused on the long term.

Motivation

Financial goals provide purpose and energy and help you stay disciplined with your budgeting process. Your goals should be important to you so that they provide inspiration for you to keep working towards them.

Accountability

Writing down your goals and being accountable for your progress (whether it is just to yourself or to some significant other person) keeps you honest about how you are progressing.

Accomplishment

Reaching your financial goals provides you with a sense of accomplishment. Celebrating significant milestones also helps with motivation to stick with your goals.

SECTION IV
SETTING FINANCIAL GOALS
Key Points to Consider

Setting financial goals is crucial for achieving long-term financial success and stability. Whether you want to save for a down payment on a house, pay off debt, or retire comfortably, having clear financial goals provides direction and motivation. Here are key points to consider when setting financial goals:

Be Precise

Instead of saying, "I want to save more money," set a specific target like, "I want to save $10,000 in the next 12 months." This makes your goal concrete and allows you to track your progress.

Don't Create Scarcity Goals

- Don't create goals that are so restrictive that you limit yourself from enjoying the fruits of your labor. Setting unattainable goals can lead to frustration and demotivation.

- Its okay to budget for things you enjoy. Just be mindful to prioritize budgeting and create goals for things you love and limit budgeting and purchasing things you don't love.

- Always consider your income, expenses, and any existing financial obligations you have when creating goals. Start small goals and gradually work your way up as you achieve them.

SECTION IV
SETTING FINANCIAL GOALS

Key Points to Consider

Establish Priority

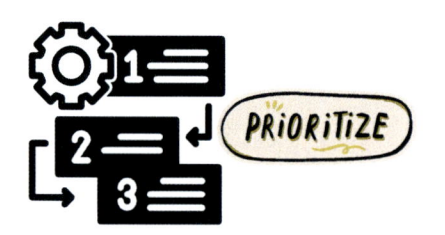

Identify what is most important to you and infuse both short-term and long-term goals on your list. This will allow you to prioritize which goal has the the highest sense of urgency and need.

Review

Regularly review and adjust your financial goals. As your circumstances change, your goals may need to be modified. Reassess your goals annually or when significant life events occur, such as a job change or starting a family.

Celebrate

Break down larger goals into smaller milestones, allowing you to celebrate achievements along the way. Take a moment to recognize the discipline and commitment that led you to your budget triumphs reinforcing positive financial habits.

> Jot down your financial goals on the provided goal planning pages. It's time well spent!

Goal Planner

GOAL
Example I would like to earn more money within the next 90 days to help pay off debts faster as my expenses are to high for my income.

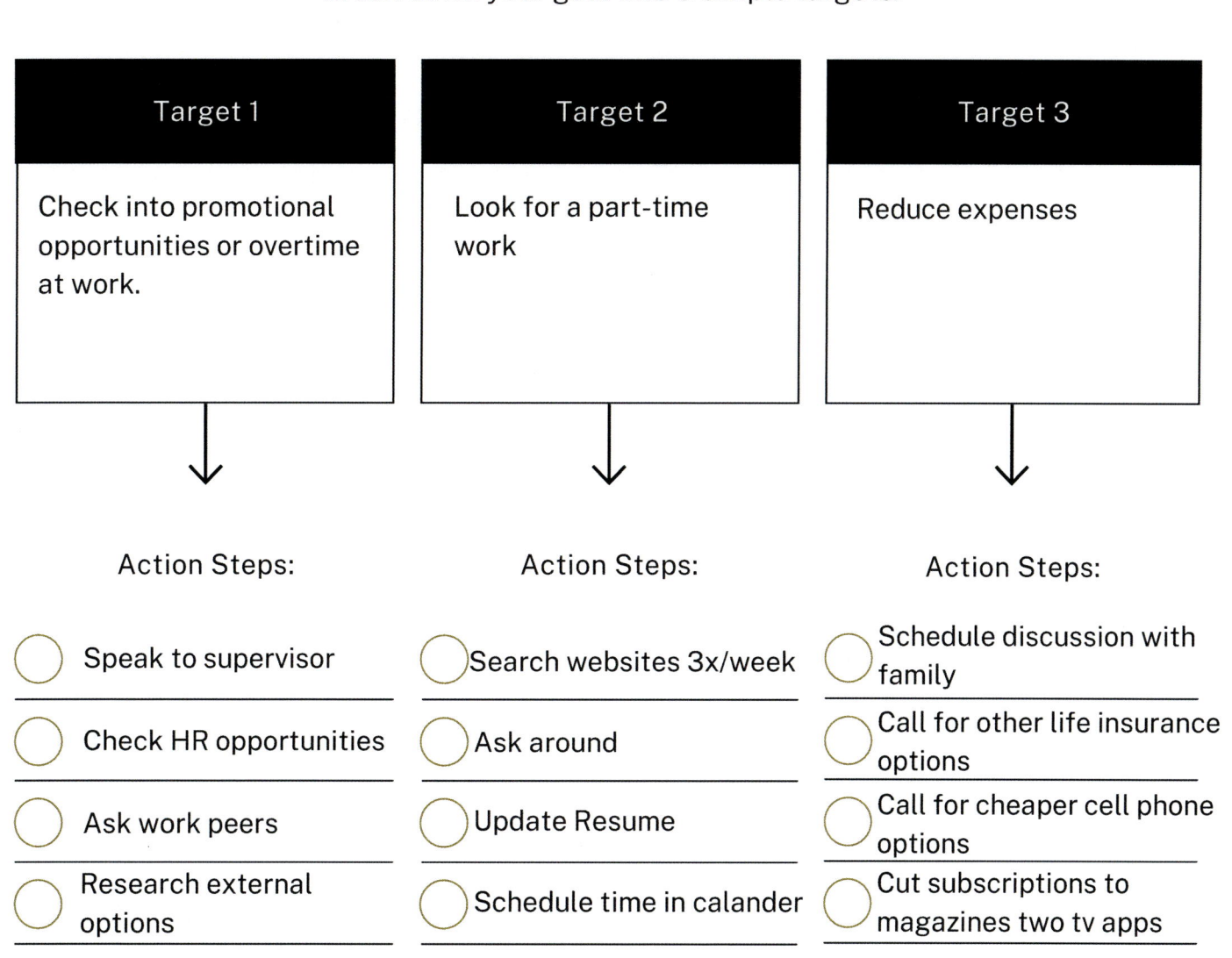

EXAMPLE

Break down your goal into 3 simple targets:

Target 1	Target 2	Target 3
Check into promotional opportunities or overtime at work.	Look for a part-time work	Reduce expenses

Action Steps:
- ◯ Speak to supervisor
- ◯ Check HR opportunities
- ◯ Ask work peers
- ◯ Research external options

Action Steps:
- ◯ Search websites 3x/week
- ◯ Ask around
- ◯ Update Resume
- ◯ Schedule time in calander

Action Steps:
- ◯ Schedule discussion with family
- ◯ Call for other life insurance options
- ◯ Call for cheaper cell phone options
- ◯ Cut subscriptions to magazines two tv apps

34

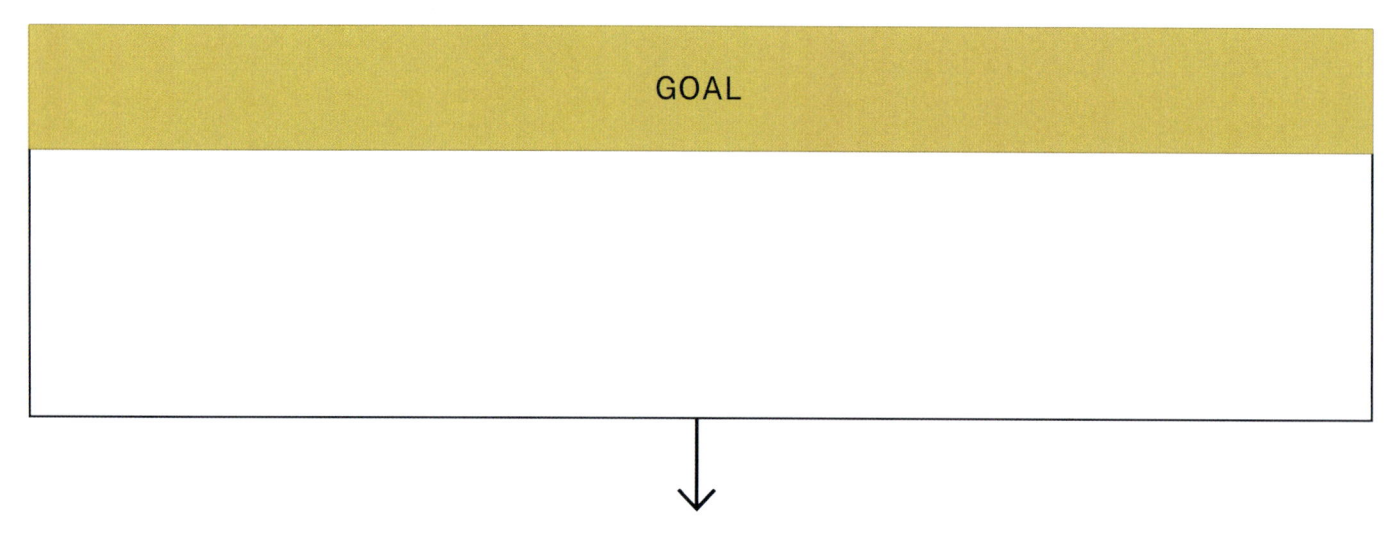

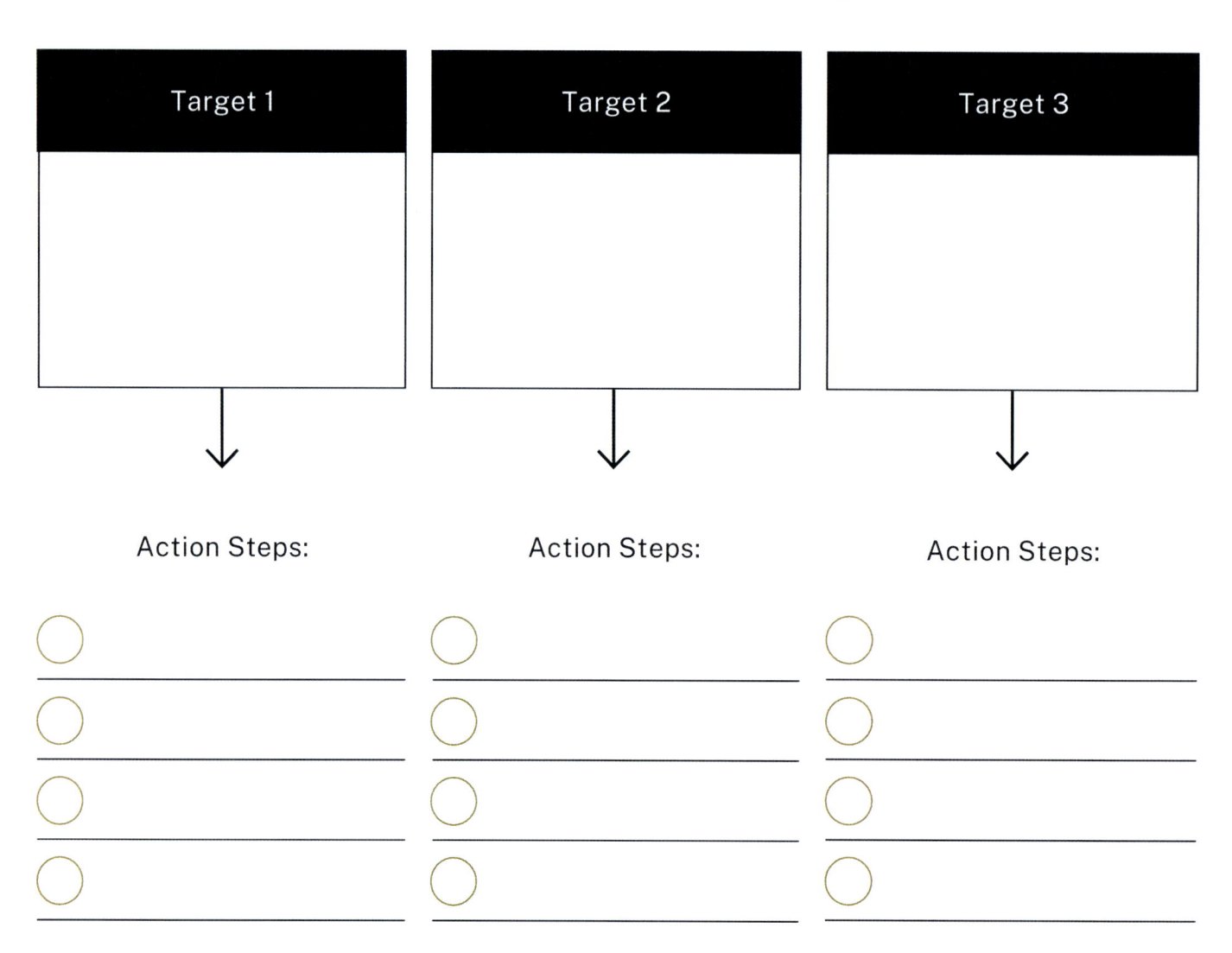

Goal Planner

GOAL

Break down your goal into 3 simple targets:

Target 1	Target 2	Target 3

Action Steps: Action Steps: Action Steps:

- ○ _____
- ○ _____
- ○ _____
- ○ _____

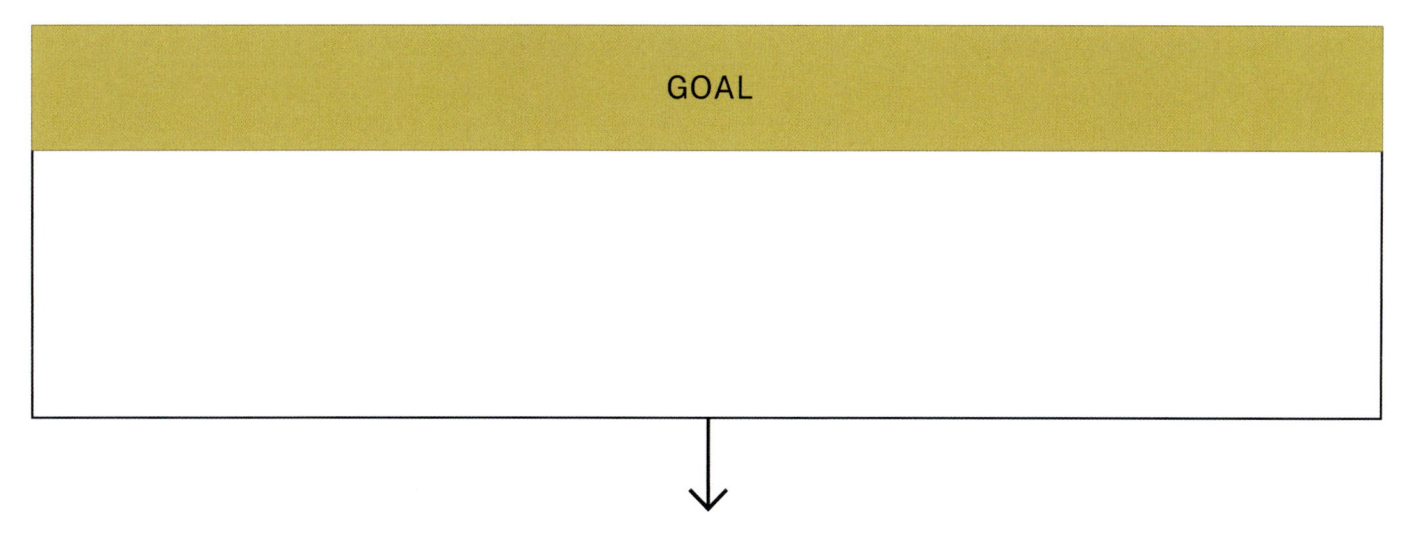

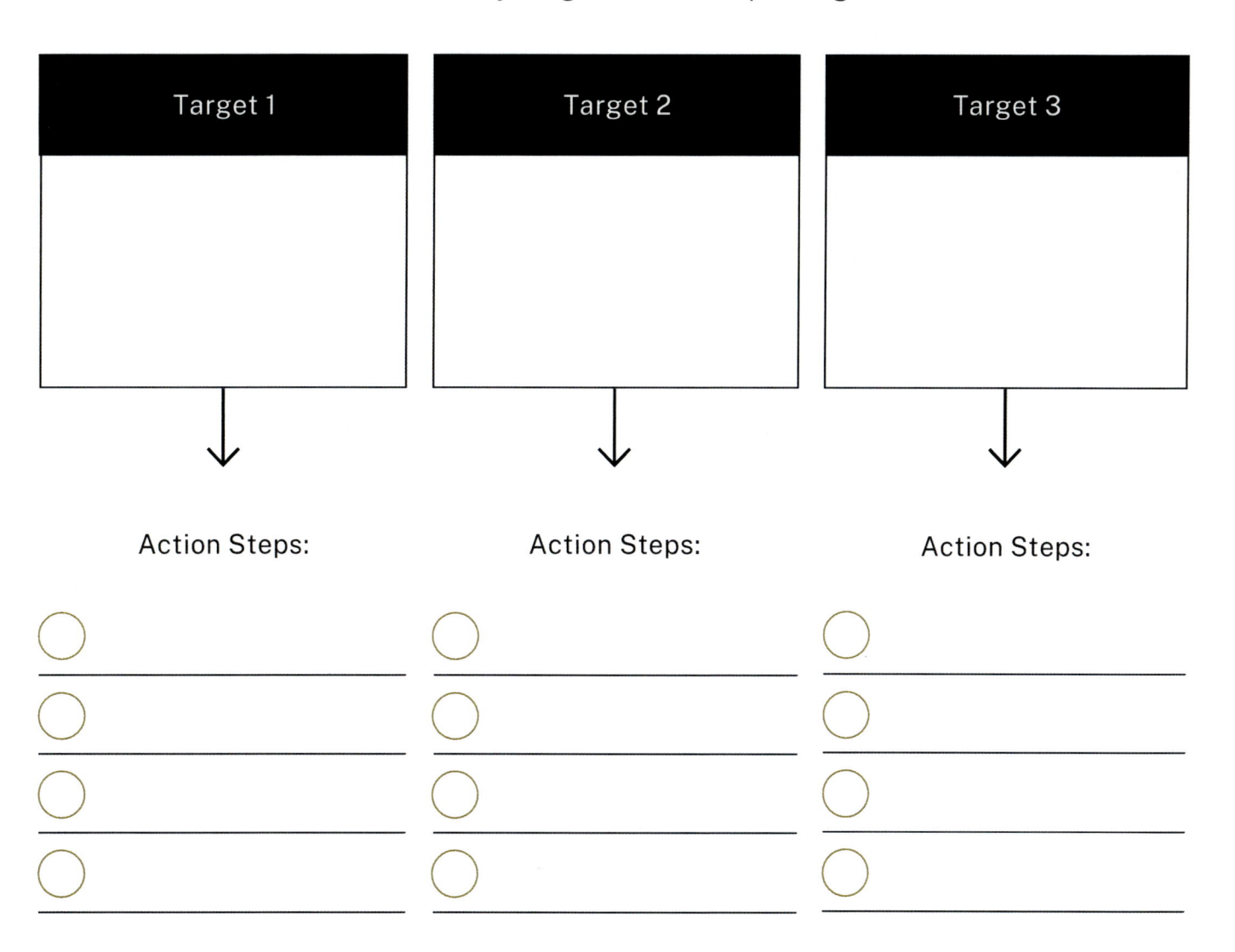

Goal Planner

GOAL

↓

Break down your goal into 3 simple targets:

Target 1	Target 2	Target 3

↓ ↓ ↓

Action Steps: Action Steps: Action Steps:

○ _____   ○ _____   ○ _____

○ _____   ○ _____   ○ _____

○ _____   ○ _____   ○ _____

○ _____   ○ _____   ○ _____

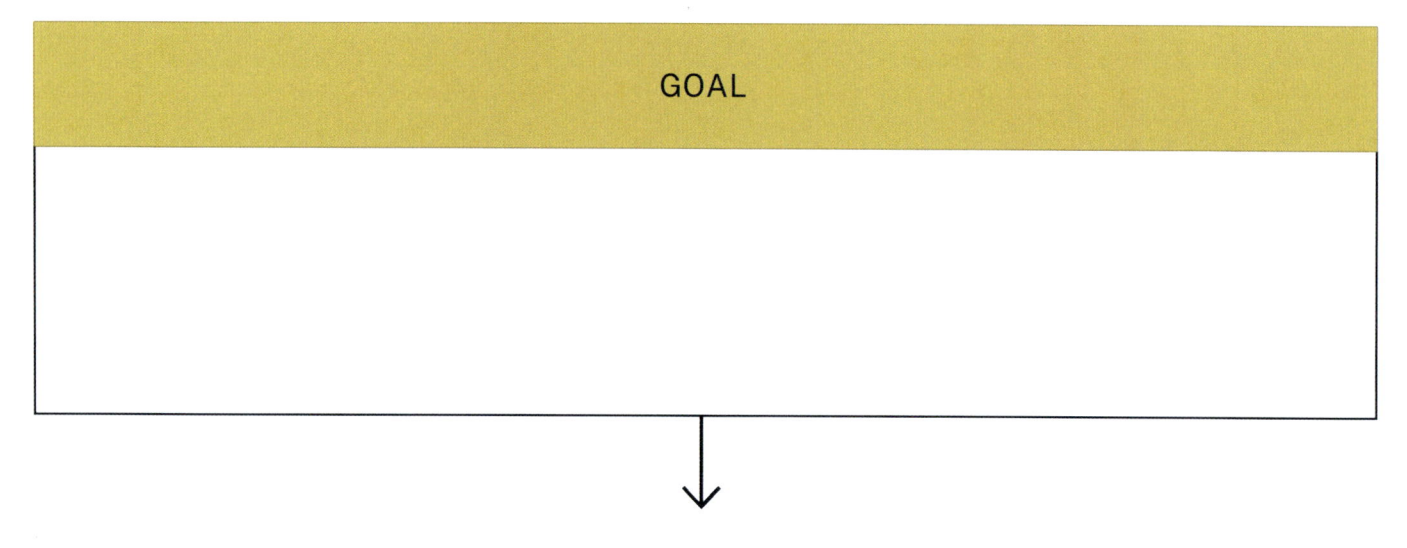

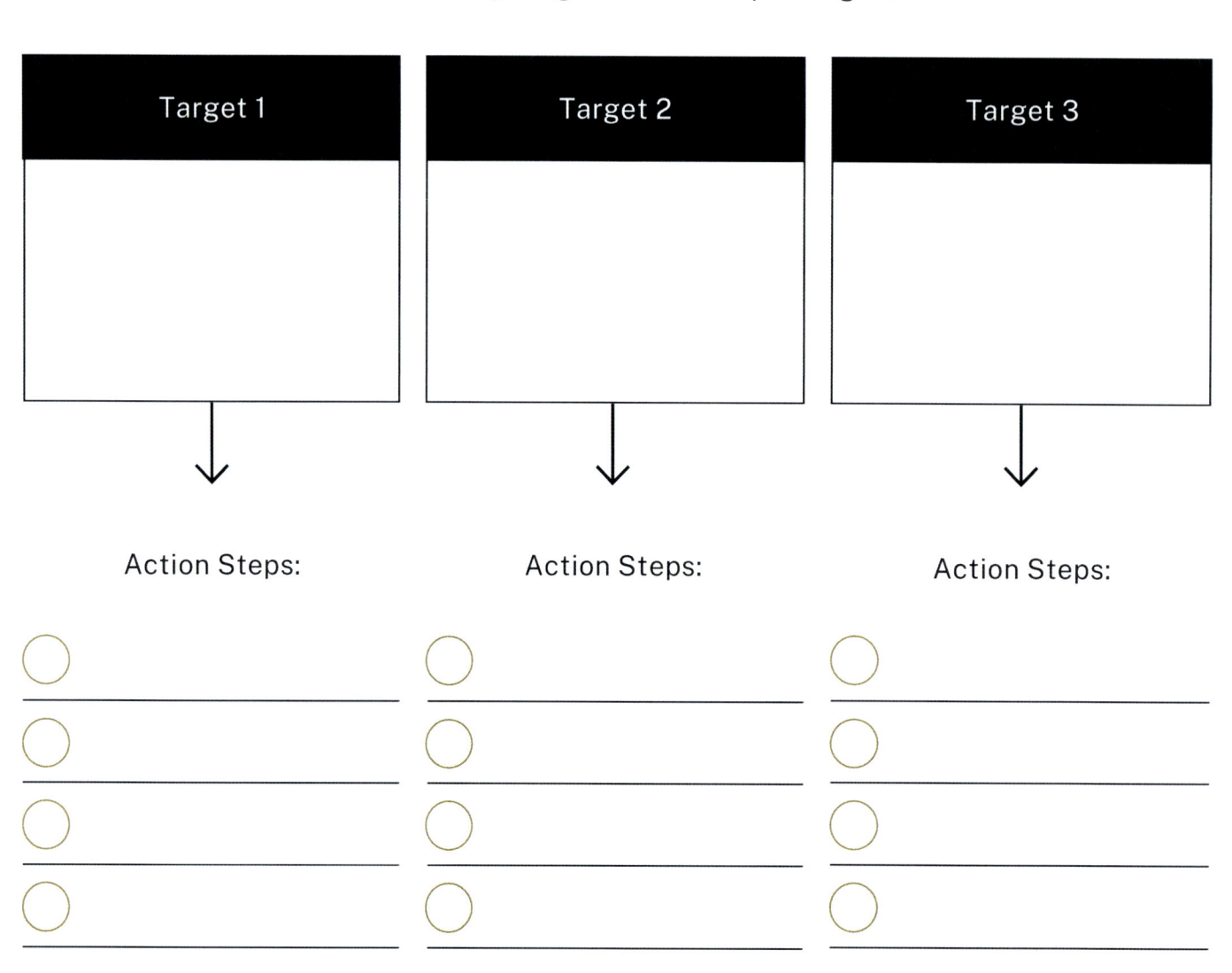

Goal Planner

GOAL

Break down your goal into 3 simple targets:

Target 1	Target 2	Target 3

Action Steps: Action Steps: Action Steps:

○ _____   ○ _____   ○ _____

○ _____   ○ _____   ○ _____

○ _____   ○ _____   ○ _____

○ _____   ○ _____   ○ _____

CONGRATULATIONS

Heartiest congratulations on reaching this milestone of completing your budget plan! Your dedication and commitment to securing your financial future deserve applause. With this achievement, you've not only created a roadmap to success but have also set the stage for turning your dreams into reality.

It's crucial to recognize that the true essence of this accomplishment lies in the consistent application of your budget. Every smart financial decision you make contributes to the realization of your goals. Remember, financial success is a journey, not a destination, and the key is to stay the course.

As you bask in the glow of this newfound financial freedom, let me remind you of the invaluable role of continual financial education. Just like a compass guides a traveler through uncharted territories, ongoing financial education empowers you to navigate the ever-evolving landscape of personal finance. Stay curious, stay informed, and let knowledge be your greatest asset.

Warren Buffett's timeless wisdom echoes in this moment: "The best investment you can make is in yourself." Your journey to financial success is not just about numbers; it's about the growth, learning, and self-investment along the way. Here's to your remarkable success, and may your financial future shine as brightly as your unwavering determination!

Abra Smith
Founder & CEO
The Melanin Project

ADDITIONAL BUDGET PLANNER SHEETS

Located on pages 40 to 50

MONTHLY
BUDGET PLANNER

NAME:

MONTH:

INCOME

INCOME SOURCES	AMOUNT

TOTAL

SAVING GOAL/EMERGENCY FUND

ITEM	AMOUNT

TOTAL

EXPENSES

EXPENSES ITEM	AMOUNT	DUE DATE

TOTAL

MONTHLY SUMMARY

TOTAL INCOME   TOTAL EXPENSES   DIFFERENCE

FAST PAYMENT   NOTES

MONTHLY
BUDGET PLANNER

NAME:

MONTH:

INCOME

INCOME SOURCES	AMOUNT
TOTAL	

SAVING GOAL/EMERGENCY FUND

ITEM	AMOUNT
TOTAL	

EXPENSES

EXPENSES ITEM	AMOUNT	DUE DATE
TOTAL		

MONTHLY SUMMARY

TOTAL INCOME	TOTAL EXPENSES	DIFFERENCE

FAST PAYMENT   **NOTES**

MONTHLY
BUDGET PLANNER

NAME:

MONTH:

INCOME

INCOME SOURCES	AMOUNT
TOTAL	

SAVING GOAL/EMERGENCY FUND

ITEM	AMOUNT
TOTAL	

EXPENSES

EXPENSES ITEM	AMOUNT	DUE DATE
	TOTAL	

MONTHLY SUMMARY

TOTAL INCOME	TOTAL EXPENSES	DIFFERENCE

FAST PAYMENT	NOTES

MONTHLY
BUDGET PLANNER

NAME:

MONTH:

INCOME

INCOME SOURCES	AMOUNT

TOTAL

SAVING GOAL/EMERGENCY FUND

ITEM	AMOUNT

TOTAL

EXPENSES

EXPENSES ITEM	AMOUNT	DUE DATE

TOTAL

MONTHLY SUMMARY

TOTAL INCOME | TOTAL EXPENSES | DIFFERENCE

FAST PAYMENT | NOTES

42

MONTHLY
BUDGET PLANNER

NAME:

MONTH:

INCOME

INCOME SOURCES	AMOUNT
TOTAL	

SAVING GOAL/EMERGENCY FUND

ITEM	AMOUNT
TOTAL	

EXPENSES

EXPENSES ITEM	AMOUNT	DUE DATE
	TOTAL	

MONTHLY SUMMARY

TOTAL INCOME	TOTAL EXPENSES	DIFFERENCE

FAST PAYMENT — **NOTES**

MONTHLY
BUDGET PLANNER

NAME:

MONTH:

INCOME

INCOME SOURCES	AMOUNT
TOTAL	

SAVING GOAL/EMERGENCY FUND

ITEM	AMOUNT
TOTAL	

EXPENSES

EXPENSES ITEM	AMOUNT	DUE DATE
TOTAL		

MONTHLY SUMMARY

TOTAL INCOME　　　**TOTAL EXPENSES**　　　**DIFFERENCE**

FAST PAYMENT　　　**NOTES**

MONTHLY
BUDGET PLANNER

NAME:

MONTH:

INCOME

INCOME SOURCES	AMOUNT
TOTAL	

SAVING GOAL/EMERGENCY FUND

ITEM	AMOUNT
TOTAL	

EXPENSES

EXPENSES ITEM	AMOUNT	DUE DATE
	TOTAL	

MONTHLY SUMMARY

TOTAL INCOME	TOTAL EXPENSES	DIFFERENCE

FAST PAYMENT   **NOTES**

MONTHLY
BUDGET PLANNER

NAME:

MONTH:

INCOME

INCOME SOURCES	AMOUNT
	TOTAL

SAVING GOAL/EMERGENCY FUND

ITEM	AMOUNT
	TOTAL

EXPENSES

EXPENSES ITEM	AMOUNT	DUE DATE
		TOTAL

MONTHLY SUMMARY

TOTAL INCOME

TOTAL EXPENSES

DIFFERENCE

FAST PAYMENT

NOTES

MONTHLY
BUDGET PLANNER

NAME:

MONTH:

INCOME

INCOME SOURCES	AMOUNT
TOTAL	

SAVING GOAL/EMERGENCY FUND

ITEM	AMOUNT
TOTAL	

EXPENSES

EXPENSES ITEM	AMOUNT	DUE DATE
TOTAL		

MONTHLY SUMMARY

TOTAL INCOME	TOTAL EXPENSES	DIFFERENCE

FAST PAYMENT	NOTES	

MONTHLY
BUDGET PLANNER

NAME:

MONTH:

INCOME

INCOME SOURCES	AMOUNT
	TOTAL

SAVING GOAL/EMERGENCY FUND

ITEM	AMOUNT
	TOTAL

EXPENSES

EXPENSES ITEM	AMOUNT	DUE DATE
	TOTAL	

MONTHLY SUMMARY

TOTAL INCOME	TOTAL EXPENSES	DIFFERENCE

FAST PAYMENT — **NOTES**

48

MONTHLY
BUDGET PLANNER

NAME:

MONTH:

INCOME

INCOME SOURCES	AMOUNT
TOTAL	

SAVING GOAL/EMERGENCY FUND

ITEM	AMOUNT
TOTAL	

EXPENSES

EXPENSES ITEM	AMOUNT	DUE DATE
TOTAL		

MONTHLY SUMMARY

TOTAL INCOME	TOTAL EXPENSES	DIFFERENCE

FAST PAYMENT	NOTES	

MONTHLY
BUDGET PLANNER

NAME:

MONTH:

INCOME

INCOME SOURCES	AMOUNT
TOTAL	

SAVING GOAL/EMERGENCY FUND

ITEM	AMOUNT
TOTAL	

EXPENSES

EXPENSES ITEM	AMOUNT	DUE DATE
TOTAL		

MONTHLY SUMMARY

TOTAL INCOME	TOTAL EXPENSES	DIFFERENCE

FAST PAYMENT

NOTES

Made in the USA
Middletown, DE
17 March 2024